Tai Chi for Kids

Move with the Animals

*Eight simple Tai Chi movements
parents can teach their children
for health, imagination, and play*

Written by Stuart Alve Olson

Illustrated by Gregory Crawford

Photography by Patrick Gross

Featuring Lee Jin Olson

Bear Cub Books

Rochester, Vermont

Bear Cub Books

One Park Street
Rochester, Vermont 05767
www.InnerTraditions.com

Bear Cub Books is a division of Bear & Company

Library of Congress Cataloging-in-Publication Data

Olson, Stuart Alve.
Tai Chi for kids : move with the animals : eight simple Tai Chi movements
parents can teach their children for health, imagination, and play / written by Stuart Alive Olson ; illustrations by Gregory Crawford.
p. cm.
Summary: Teaches the basics of the ancient Chinese exercise of Tai Chi through a
story, illustrations, and simple, step-by-step directions.
ISBN 1-879181-65-7
1. Tai chi for children—Juvenile literature. [1. Tai chi. 2. Martial arts.]
I. Crawford, Gregory, ill. II. Title.

GV504.6.C44 O57 2001
613.7'148—dc21
2001043138

Printed and bound in China

10 9 8 7 6 5 4 3 2 1

Text design and layout by Gregory Crawford
This book was typeset in Palatino and Comic Sans with Parchment for the display typeface
The illustrations in this book were done in pen-and-ink with watercolor and colored pencil on 90 lb. Arches watercolor paper

To my Golden Rooster son, Lee Jin.
Thank you for showing me how to teach children.
You are unquestionably the greatest joy in my life.

Lil' Jonathan and Patrick, this book should finally make Tai Chi fun and clear for both of you.
When you both learn to play, imagination can become reality.

Contents

Tai Chi Is for Children

As a parent, I understand not only the desire but the need for my child to play and use his imagination. For children, playing is a fun way of learning that helps them develop social and behavioral skills. Tai Chi—even for adults—is based on playfulness and making full use of the imagination.

During my many years of teaching Tai Chi to adults, my students and other parents would ask me if I could teach their children too, but I always said no. Not because I didn't want to, but because I thought teaching children traditional disciplines of Tai Chi would be just too boring for them. This all changed, however, when my three-year-old son taught *me* how to teach kids.

This happened following an event at the 1996 Festival of Nations in St. Paul, Minnesota, where several of my adult students and I were demonstrating Tai Chi. Just after we had finished and the audience began clapping, my young son, Lee Jin, darted out behind us and began doing a Tai Chi posture from the form Dragon Plays in the Clouds. This was a complete surprise. I had never taught him how to do this, but there he was mimicking the movement perfectly, and, of course, he got a bigger round of applause than we did.

From that day on Lee Jin wanted to learn more postures, not the form as a whole (all of the movements in the correct order), just individual postures. My son's insistence on being taught in this manner made me feel quite foolish, because, in fact, this is exactly how Tai Chi first developed—with eight postures done separately, much like a *kata* in karate.

太极

How could *I*, with my background and experience, have missed such an obvious solution to teaching kids Tai Chi? Since then, having taught my son as well as many other children, I have learned four important lessons:

1. *Children love the idea of playing with or pretending to be animals.*
Because the Tai Chi movements are based on animals, children are drawn to this practice. Giving kids the opportunity to express the movements of imaginary animals helps them develop their own creativity.

2. *Kids love to show other children how to perform specific movements.*
Children love to teach what they've learned to others. It gives them a true sense of self-confidence and self-worth.

3. *Kids laugh incessantly while learning.*
Studies have shown that children *need* to laugh, and healthy children do so about three hundred times a day. Tai Chi does not require children to be solemn and serious while they are learning the movements or while they are performing their practice. Tai Chi can be very joyful and the learning of Tai Chi can be very fun.

4. *Children really do crave disciplined play, especially when their parents help them.*
Parents should never underestimate how much their kids want them to learn and play along with them—as long as the parent remembers to play and not dictate grown-up perceptions of perfection.

Parents will be glad to know that practicing Tai Chi provides numerous health, learning, and social benefits. Imitating or moving

太極

with the Tai Chi animals will help your child develop his or her imagination and creative skills. A regular practice of Tai Chi develops children's ability to focus on what they are doing, increasing their overall attention span and ability to concentrate. It also helps them enhance their breathing and motor skills.

On a physical level, research has shown that Tai Chi strengthens equilibrium. Interestingly, children and seniors share the difficulties of an unstable sense of balance, and studies done by the American Association of Retired Persons (AARP) prove that seniors who practice Tai Chi develop a strong sense of balance. For children, practicing Tai Chi helps develop their central equilibrium early on. Because Tai Chi improves circulation, it can strengthen the immune system and prevent osteoporosis. Tai Chi has been shown by

the Arthritis Foundation to be one of the best cures for arthritis, a condition that can affect both children and adults. Considering such proven health benefits, there is no question that Tai Chi is equally as beneficial for children's health as it is for adults.

Tai Chi is low impact, so parents need not worry about their child injuring joints or muscles from the high-impact activity of some other forms of exercise.

Although Tai Chi is intended for self-defense, it is not the type of self-defense normally associated with martial arts. In Tai Chi, *self-defense* means "defense against yourself." Tai Chi supports the fact that in any situation in which you might get hurt, whether from an attack or by simply falling, it is important not to further the injury through your own mistakes. "Defending against the self" ranges in meaning from

太極

not putting yourself in situations of harm in the first place to keeping yourself from making it worse when you do.

In a world that is growing ever more violent, our children are inundated with images of aggressiveness, from television wrestlers to the evening news, as well as video games and cartoons. The answer to ensuring that our children do not grow up with violent tendencies lies not in teaching them how to fight but in teaching them that they can protect themselves. Teaching them to fight only serves to confirm in their young minds that violence is acceptable. A better direction is found in teaching them how not to get hurt, how to yield, how to be aware of their environment so that they have self-confidence and understanding that violence is ignorance, and that real strength comes from an awareness of both themselves and their surroundings.

Like all good parents I want desperately for my child to develop self-confidence and a sense of self-worth that is tempered with humility. Tai Chi can provide one huge step for your child in that direction. It instills values of nonaggression, playfulness, and humility within its practice and teaching. Studying and practicing Tai Chi with your child will also strengthen their trust and friendship with you.

Like most children's books, this book has as much value for the adult as for the child. My sincere hope is that this book will teach children and adults how to play and imagine. Young or old, we all need to experience our inner child, to exercise our imagination, and to just play. Good health is always rooted in a bright smile and laughter. May this book bring both to you and your child.

A Story about Tai Chi

A very long time ago there was a Chinese monk who loved nature. Because he lived in some mountains that had three high peaks, he named himself "Three Peaks Chang." Every day he would take nature walks, study his books, and sit very quietly in meditation, listening to his breath and the sounds of nature.

One day, when Three Peaks Chang was sitting in his small hut, he heard loud noises outside. It was a bird squawking and a snake hissing. He got up, looked out, and saw that the bird was trying to catch the snake, and the snake was trying to get away. Three Peaks Chang was curious to see how the snake would get away from the bird, so he watched them carefully from just outside his hut.

The bird would swoop down at the snake, but every time the snake would just wiggle and turn out of the way. When the bird tried to peck the snake's tail, the snake would chase the bird away by striking with its head. When the bird tried to peck the snake's head, the tail of the snake would push the bird away. When the bird tried to peck the middle of the snake, both the snake's head and tail would swish at the bird.

This went on for a long time, and eventually the bird got tired and flew away. The snake then slept in the sun.

Three Peaks Chang was very impressed by what he saw, and he thought how wonderful it would be if only he could be as relaxed and wiggly as the snake, then nothing could hurt him.

After thinking about the movements of these two animals for a while, Three Peaks Chang thought about the movements of other animals as well, and he created eight different exercises, based on animal movements and postures, which he named "Tai Chi." The amazing thing he discovered was that the more he did the exercises the healthier he became. Bandits he met in the mountains no longer bothered him, and wild animals no longer attacked him.

Why do you think this was? Well, it was because Tai Chi made him soft and gentle, just like water. If you throw a rock into the water, the rock just sinks and disappears. Rocks cannot hurt water. Three Peaks Chang learned to hurt nothing, and so nothing would hurt him. This is a wonderful thing to know, and you can learn it too by doing Tai Chi.

Three Peaks Chang lived a very long time and was very healthy and happy, so much so that news spread about him all over China. The news was so great that the emperor wanted to give him a job and learn Tai Chi from him. But Three Peaks Chang refused. He just wanted to live in the mountains and do Tai Chi so he could remain healthy and happy forever.

Come and Learn Tai Chi

太极

Tai Chi, pronounced "tie jee," is a very old exercise first invented in China. Millions of children and grown-ups practice Tai Chi every day. You can do Tai Chi anywhere—in your house, in your yard, in the park, or even when you're waiting for the school bus. The eight Tai Chi animal forms in this book are some of the most fun and healthy you can do.

Even though Tai Chi is one of the martial arts, Tai Chi is not used for fighting. Tai Chi teaches you how to get out of the way of trouble by being in control of your body in a gentle and relaxed way. People who like to fight are like sticks—they get broken. People who are soft and relaxed just bend and turn and don't get hurt.

Think of a cat. A cat moves in a Tai Chi-like way—it looks relaxed and slow at times, but it is very alert and fast when it wants to be. Have you ever seen a cat catch a mouse or watched it play with a ball of string? Cats are very fast, yet very relaxed. They are

太極

in control. Or think of a stream. Water is the gentlest and yet strongest thing in the world. Water flows around anything that gets in its way, but it never fights with anything. Tai Chi is like flowing water.

If you want to become really good at Tai Chi you must do it every day. Remember when you learned to brush your teeth or tie your shoes? You became really good at those things because you did them every day. To get really good at something, you must repeat it every day. Birds fly so well because they do it every day. Fish swim so well because they do it every day. So remember to do Tai Chi every day, and one day you will see that you are very good at it.

When you are good at Tai Chi you'll be very happy and healthy.

How to Perform the Tai Chi Movements in This Book

太極

Tai Chi movements are meant to be slow and fluid—like water. Although the photographs in this book divide the forms into separate steps, your goal is not to "land" in a particular position, but rather to glide from one step to another in one continuous motion. You do Tai Chi slowly to feel calm and to make sure your feet and body are balanced, even as you shift weight from one side to another. If you go too fast you might lose your balance.

The starting position for each posture is standing upright with your feet apart and your arms hanging down loose and relaxed at your sides. Before you begin moving, breathe in and out several times to help you relax. As you begin moving, continue to breathe naturally; don't hold your breath or try to control the speed of your breathing. If you just breathe in a gentle and normal way the Tai Chi movements will feel really natural and easy.

Once you learn the movements you should repeat them over and over. It is best to repeat the postures at least eight times. When you finish all the steps in the posture, move back to the neutral starting position and begin all over again. Don't stop between repetitions, just keep moving in a fluid way until you have performed all the movements eight times in a row. Later on, when you feel you can

太極

do the movements easily and not forget where to step and turn, you should teach yourself to do the postures starting on the opposite side. For example, in Holding a Bird's Tail you first shift your weight onto your LEFT leg and turn to the RIGHT. When you are ready to do the opposite side, you will shift on to your RIGHT leg and begin turning LEFT. Once you have learned and mastered the postures as they are described in this book, it will be easy perform them on the opposite side. By doing the postures on both sides, you build a stronger, more energetic, and healthy body.

Doing Tai Chi to music makes the movements much easier to perform and a lot more fun too. Music can help us relax, focus, and slow down while doing Tai Chi. There is a lot of good music that can complement the gentle rhythms of Tai Chi and even inspire thoughts of the particular animals and gestures. You will have to experiment to find the music you like best. When my son and I do Tai Chi together we like to use the theme song from the movie THE LAST EMPEROR. Instrumental music is generally less distracting than vocal music, making concentration and movement easier.

Holding the Bird's Tail

You must be very gentle in order to hold a bird in your hands. One hand must cup the front of the bird's chest, and the other hand must caress its back and tail. Can you imagine you are holding a bird so gently but steadily that it cannot fly away?

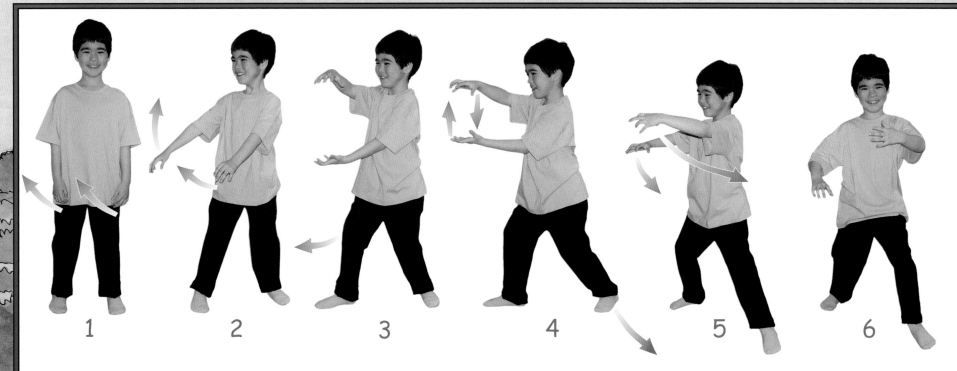

1   2   3   4   5   6

Stand with your feet apart and your arms hanging down (step 1). Let your shoulders relax and feel the breath at the bottom of your stomach.

Next, turn at the waist to your RIGHT as you point your RIGHT foot. Shift all your weight onto your RIGHT leg as you bring your hands up to catch the bird before it flies away (step 2). Your RIGHT hand touches the top of the bird's head and your LEFT hand is underneath on the front of the bird's

chest (step 3). You should feel like you are holding a big ball in your hands.

Now with your LEFT foot, take one step out to the side. Your weight stays on your RIGHT foot and your body is still facing the RIGHT. At the same time that you move your LEFT foot, raise your LEFT hand and arm so that they are in front of your chest (step 4). Imagine that you are picking up the bird as your LEFT arm moves up. You should feel like you are holding a big

ball to your chest with your arm. As your LEFT hand moves up your RIGHT hand moves out to the side and down as if you were sliding it down the bird's back to its tail (step 5).

To finish, turn your waist to the LEFT and sit down a little bit so there is weight also in your LEFT leg and hold the bird. Your LEFT hand is embracing the bird's chest, and your RIGHT hand is holding the bird's tail (step 6). Repeat eight times on each side.

17

Snake Slithering Down

Snakes are really quiet. When they slide down a rock or hill you can't hear them. They are really wiggly and move slowly and gracefully. Can you slide down and slither just like a snake?

18

1

2

3

4

5

Stand with your feet apart and your arms hanging down (step 1). Let your shoulders relax and feel the breath at the bottom of your stomach.

Step way back with your RIGHT foot and then sit down as low as you can, with all your weight on your RIGHT leg. At the same time raise your LEFT hand up and over in a circle until it is in front of your body with your palm facing down and raise your RIGHT arm out to the side with your fingers curled downward like a snake's tail (step 2).

Keep your RIGHT arm extended as your LEFT hand moves back and down to imitate the head of the snake. Turn your waist and body to follow the movement of your LEFT arm, but keep your weight on your RIGHT leg. Your LEFT hand moves down to your stomach level (step 3).

Now turn your waist and body to the RIGHT with the weight still on your your RIGHT leg. Slide your LEFT arm forward until the back of your LEFT hand is on your inner thigh, imitating

the head of the snake moving forward (step 4).

Shifting your weight forward onto your LEFT leg, bring your LEFT arm and hand slightly upward, like a snake lifting its head, until your fingers point diagonally at the ground (step 5).

Repeat entire pattern eight times on each side.

White Crane Cools Its Wings

White cranes are big beautiful birds.
When they get too warm they open
their wings and flap them to cool off.
Can you cool off like a white crane too?

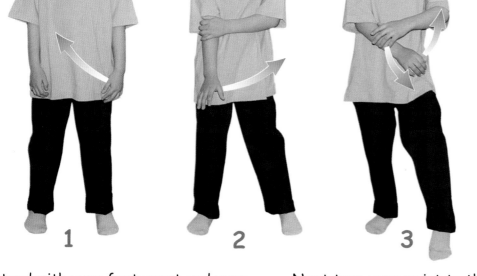

1

2

3

4

5

Stand with your feet apart and your arms hanging down (step 1). Let your shoulders relax and feel the breath at the bottom of your stomach.

Shift your weight onto your RIGHT leg and bring your LEFT hand over to touch the top of your RIGHT elbow (step 2). As you do this, turn your waist to the RIGHT

Next turn your waist to the front and point your LEFT foot forward (step 3). At the same time bring your RIGHT arm over your LEFT arm and point your LEFT hand downward (step 4), just like a crane crosses its wings before it spreads them wide open.

Now spread your arms open wide. Your RIGHT hand goes up over your head

with your palm facing out. Your LEFT hand moves over to the LEFT side of your body with your palm facing down (step 5). You should feel like a crane bringing its RIGHT wing up and fanning out its LEFT wing to cool itself.

Repeat entire pattern eight times on each side.

Carry the Tiger Back to the Mountain

When a tiger comes down from a mountain all the people worry and hide in their houses. They want someone to take the tiger back to the mountain where it lives. Can you carry the tiger back to the mountain?

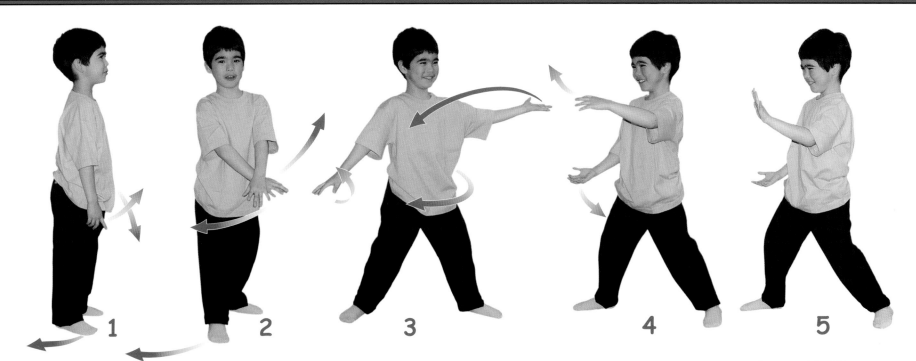

Stand with your feet apart and your arms hanging down (step 1). Let your shoulders relax and feel the breath at the bottom of your stomach.

Bend your LEFT knee slightly, putting your weight on your LEFT leg. Turn your waist to the RIGHT and point your RIGHT foot forward (keep your weight on your LEFT leg). At the same time raise your hands so they cross at the wrists, pointing diagonally downward (step 2).

With your RIGHT foot step back on a diagonal and move your RIGHT hand back over your RIGHT leg with your palm facing down. Your LEFT arm stretches out to the side with the palm facing up (step 3). If you started step 1 as though you were facing North, you would now be facing East.

Lean into your RIGHT leg. Sweep your LEFT hand in front of your body with your palm facing down, as you bring your RIGHT hand to your RIGHT hip with the palm facing up (step 4). Imagine picking up the tiger's hind legs with your RIGHT hand. The tiger's front paws rest on top of your LEFT arm (step 5).

To finish, rise off your LEFT leg putting all the weight into your RIGHT leg. You are now ready to start walking forward to take the tiger back to the mountain. Instead, slide your LEFT leg next to your RIGHT and lower your arms (as in step 1) so you can start the movements again from this new position.

Repeat entire pattern eight times on each side.

Dragon Plays in the Clouds

Dragons like to hide and play in the clouds, and they like to take rides in them too. The clouds are like big soft pillows that they hold on to and roll around in. Can you be a dragon and hold a big, round billowy cloud in your arms and play with it like a ball?

1

2

3

4

5

Stand with your feet apart and your arms hanging down (step 1). Let your shoulders relax and feel the breath at the bottom of your stomach.

Bring your arms up, palms inward, so that your RIGHT arm is in front of your chest and your LEFT hand is in front of your stomach (step 2).

Turn your waist as far as you can to the RIGHT, and then turn the palms of your hands so they face each other (step 3) as you bend your knees. Pretend you are a dragon holding clouds within your claws.

Next, turn to the front, turning your hands over so that your LEFT hand is now in front of your chest, your RIGHT hand in front of your stomach (step 4).

To finish, turn your waist as far as you can to the LEFT and turn the palms of your hands to face each other (step 5) as you bend your knees again. Keep rotating from side to side and turning your hands over; then you will be just like a dragon playing in the clouds.

Repeat entire pattern eight times.

Wild Goose Flies Away

Have you ever seen a goose fly away? Geese don't just take off and fly straight up. No, they always flap their wings and fly off at an angle, because they are so big. They have to spread their big wings as much as possible and flap them hard to take off. Can you open your arms wide and pretend to fly off like a wild goose?

1   2   3   4   5

Stand with your feet apart and your arms hanging down (step 1). Let your shoulders relax and feel the breath at the bottom of your stomach.

Bend your LEFT knee and put your weight on your LEFT leg while you move your RIGHT leg out and back for a wider stance. Place your RIGHT hand over your LEFT hand with the palms facing each other, as if holding a small

ball in front of you (step 2). Turning to the RIGHT from the waist up, gently press your hands together (step 3).

Shifting all your weight onto your RIGHT leg, open your arms like a goose spreading its wings to fly. Your RIGHT arm moves to the RIGHT, palm up, as your waist turns to the RIGHT to follow your arm. Your LEFT hand moves back, palm down, to waist level (step 4).

To finish, squat down just slightly like a wild goose getting ready to fly away with its wings spread wide (step 5). Slide your LEFT leg next to your RIGHT and lower your arms (as in step 1) so you can start the movements again from your new position.

Repeat entire pattern eight times on each side.

Chasing the Monkeys Away

Monkeys are very playful and curious, so they can sometimes be very naughty. They are very difficult to keep off you. But they are too wily to catch, so sometimes it is better to just move back from them and brush them away. Can you chase the monkeys away?

1

2

3

4

Stand with your feet apart and your arms hanging down (step 1). Let your shoulders relax and feel the breath at the bottom of your stomach.

Step back with your RIGHT foot. Bring your LEFT hand to the front with the palm down, and bring your RIGHT hand back with the palm facing up. Turn your waist slightly to the RIGHT as you open your arms (step 2). Spreading your arms wide makes you look bigger to the

monkeys, so they want to run away. Your LEFT hand moves as if you were putting it on the head of a monkey in front of you while you move your RIGHT hand back to brush away another monkey behind you.

Turn your waist to the front and shift all your weight onto your RIGHT leg. At the same time bend your LEFT elbow to bring your LEFT hand (palm up) back alongside your LEFT hip, and bring your

RIGHT hand up and over your head to the front of your body with your palm facing out (step 3). Imagine that you are telling the monkeys to stop.

To finish, rise up on your RIGHT foot, and at the same time move your RIGHT hand out forward (step 4) to keep the monkey from coming any closer.

Repeat eight times on each side.

Golden Rooster Stands on One Leg

Roosters stand on one leg when they rest. They are so still and so quiet that you might think they are just statues. How do they do this? First of all, they don't lean backward, forward, or to the side. The rooster lets its foot be as relaxed as a wet mop and then lets its whole body sink. Can you stand on one leg as relaxed and quiet as a rooster?

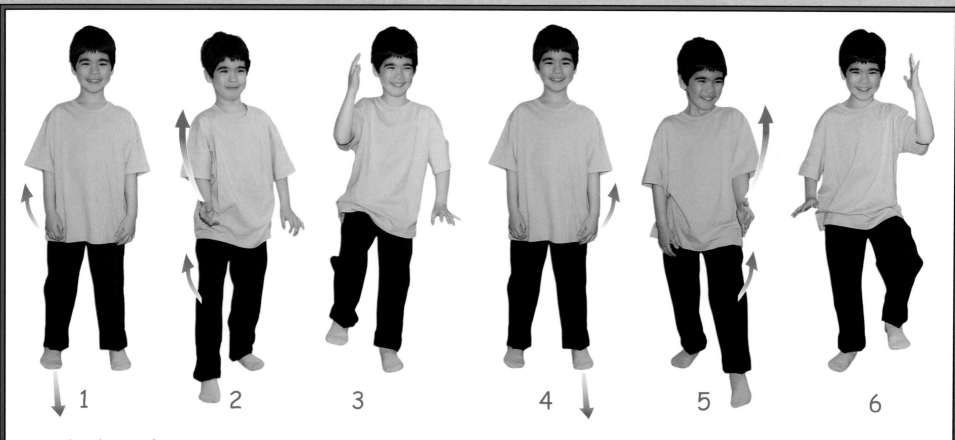

1

2

3

4

5

6

Stand with your feet apart and your arms hanging down (step 1). Let your shoulders relax and feel the breath at the bottom of your stomach.

Shift all your weight onto your LEFT leg. Point your RIGHT foot forward and raise your RIGHT arm to be even with your RIGHT foot. Your fingers should be pointing at the ground (step 2).

Next, raise your RIGHT leg so your thigh is parallel with the ground. At the same time raise your RIGHT arm so your elbow is directly over your knee and your fingers point straight up (step 3). Stand like this and count to three, or maybe even ten. Now try to relax and stand very still, like a rooster resting on one leg.

To finish, you can put your leg down and stand in the starting position (step 1 and also step 4) and do the same movement with your LEFT leg and LEFT arm (steps 5 and 6), like a rooster changing legs to sleep on.

Repeat eight times on each side.

About the Author

The author and his son, Lee Jin Olson.

Stuart Alve Olson has studied Tai Chi, meditation, and Chinese language for more than twenty-five years. Considered one of the leading authorities on Tai Chi, Stuart has published a number of books on the subject and has taught classes and workshops throughout the United States, Canada, Hong Kong, and Indonesia. He presently lives in northern California.

Stuart can be reached by e-mail at yitaichi@mediaone.net or by mail in care of the publisher.